# PROUD TO BE Muslim

Made in United States
Troutdale, OR
04/04/2024

18932772R00076